Ancient Civilizations Bingo Book

COMPLETE BINGO GAME IN A BOOK

Written By Rebecca Stark

ISBN 978-0-87386-456-5

Educational Books 'n' Bingo

Printed in the U.S.A.

ANCIENT CIVILIZATIONS BINGO
Directions

INCLUDED:

List of Terms

Templates for Additional Terms and Clues

2 Clues per Term

30 Unique Bingo Cards

Markers

1. **Either cut apart the book or make copies of ALL the sheets. You might want to make an extra copy of the clue sheets to use for introduction and review. Keep the sheets in an envelope for easy reuse.**

2. Cut apart the call cards with terms and clues.

3. Pass out one bingo card per student. There are enough for a class of 30.

4. Pass out markers. You may cut apart the markers included in this book or use any other small items of your choice.

5. Decide whether or not you will require the entire card to be filled. Requiring the entire card to be filled provides a better review. However, if you have a short time to fill, you may prefer to have them do the just the border or some other format. Tell the class before you begin what is required.

6. There are 50 topics. Read the list before you begin. If there are any topics that have not been covered in class, you may want to read to the students the topic and clues before you begin.

7. There is a blank space in the middle of each card. You can instruct the students to use it as a free space or you can write in answers to cover topics not included. Of course, in this case you would create your own clues. (Templates provided.)

8. Shuffle the cards and place them in a pile. Two or three clues are provided for each topic. If you plan to play the game with the same group more than once, you might want to choose a different clue for each game. If not, you may choose to use more than one clue.

9. Be sure to keep the cards you have used for the present game in a separate pile. When a student calls, "Bingo," he or she will have to verify that the correct answers are on his or her card AND that the markers were placed in response to the proper questions. Pull out the cards that are on the student's card keeping them in the order they were used in the game. Read each clue as it was given and ask the student to identify the correct answer from his or her card.

10. If the student has the correct answers on the card AND has shown that they were marked in response to the *correct questions,* then that student is the winner and the game is over. If the student does not have the correct answers on the card OR he or she marked the answers in response to *the wrong questions,* then the game continues until there is a proper winner.

11. If you want to play again, reshuffle the cards and begin again.

Have fun!

TERMS INCLUDED

Aphrodite

Acropolis

Aqueducts

Archeology

Artifacts

Athena

Athens

Augustus

Aztec

Book of the Dead

Chichén-Itzá

Circus

City-state

Colosseum

Confucius

Dynasties

Egypt

Forbidden City

Gladiators

Great Wall of China

Greece

Hieroglyphics (Hieroglyphs)

Homer

Inca

Maya

Mesoamerican

Mesopotamia

Mythology

Mummification

Nile River

Norse

Olympian Gods

Olympic Games

Osiris

Parthenon

Persephone

Pharaoh

Philosopher(s)

Polytheistic

Pompeii

Poseidon (and Neptune)

Pyramids

Quetzalcoatl

Ra

Roman Forum

Song Dynasty

Terracotta Army

Thor

Trojan War

Zeus

© **Barbara M. Peller**

Additional Terms

Choose as many Ancient Civilizations terms as you would like and write them in the squares. Repeat each as desired. Cut out the squares and randomly distribute them to the class. Instruct the students to place the square on the center space of their card.

Ancient Civilizations Bingo

Clues for Additional Terms

Write three clues for each of your Ancient Civilizations terms.

_____ 1. 2. 3.	_____ 1. 2. 3.
_____ 1. 2. 3.	_____ 1. 2. 3.
_____ 1. 2. 3.	_____ 1. 2. 3.

Aphrodite

1. She was the ancient Greek goddess of love and beauty.

2. The ancient Roman equivalent of this Greek goddess was Venus.

Acropolis

1. The term ___ means "upper city." The one in Athens is the most famous and is usually capitalized.

2. The Parthenon in Athens is located on the ___.

Aqueducts

1. They were built by the Romans throughout the empire to bring water to the inhabitants.

2. Built by the ancient Romans, they are considered great architectural feats.

Archeology

1. It is the systematic study of past life and culture.

2. This science is based upon the recovery and examination of material evidence of ancient cultures.

Artifacts

1. They are man-made objects. Archeologists look for them to give them clues about past cultures.

2. The discovery of Tutankhamen's tomb provided a wealth of ___. They taught us a lot about ancient Egypt.

Athena

1. She was the patron goddess of Athens.

2. This ancient Greek goddess was goddess of wisdom, war and weaving. Her Roman equivalent was Minerva.

Athens

1. Pericles was a great statesman of ___. During his reign the city-state reached its highest levels.

2. Athena was the patron goddess of this city-state.

Augustus

1. His name was Octavian, but he chose to be called ___. The Roman Empire began when he became Rome's first emperor.

2. The Roman Empire flourished under his 41-year rule.

Aztec

1. The ___ Empire was conquered by Hernan Cortez & his men in 1519.

2. Moctezuma II was ruler of the ___ Empire. Tenochtitlán was the capital city.

Book of the Dead

1. It is the name of the Egyptian funerary text.

2. It described the Egyptian concept of an afterlife and contained spells and other instructions for the deceased person's journey to the afterlife.

Ancient Civilizations Bingo

© Barbara M. Peller

Chichén-Itzá

1. These ancient Mayan ruins are in Mexico's Yucatán Peninsula.

2. Between 800 and 1200 CE it was the political, religious and military center of the Maya. These ruins are on the New 7 Wonders of the World list.

Circus

1. Chariot races took place here.

2. ___ Maximus was the site where the religious festival known as *Ludi Romani,* or Roman games, took place.

City-state

1. The ancient Greeks' loyalty was to their ___. They called it a *polis.*

2. Athens was a ___ of ancient Greece. So was Sparta.

Colosseum

1. This Roman amphitheater can hold 50,000 spectators.

2. Events held here included gladiator exhibitions and animal fights between different kinds of animals and also between humans and animals.

Confucius

1. This Chinese philosopher lived from 551 to 479 BCE.

2. His teachings stressed the importance of morality.

Dynasties

1. Periods of time during which a land is ruled by the same family are called ___.

2. Periods of time in ancient China and ancient Egypt are both referred to in terms of ___.

Egypt

1. Horus, Osiris, Isis and Set are all gods in the mythology of ancient ___.

2. The colossal sculpture known as the Great Sphinx has a human head and the body of a lion. It is located next to the Pyramids of Giza in ___.

Forbidden City

1. It was home to the emperor and his household from the Ming Dynasty through the Qing Dynasty.

2. The __ is in Beijing. It is so named because no one could enter or leave without permission from the emperor.

Gladiators

1. Often slaves or combats, they were trained to fight in mortal combat in ancient Rome.

2. They entertained the public by fighting other __ as well as wild animals.

Great Wall of China

1. It was built in stages and is more than 4,000 miles long.

2. The structure that is know known as the ___ was begun to keep Mongol nomads out of China.

Ancient Civilizations Bingo

Greece

1. Athens, Sparta and Corinth were city-states of ancient ___.

2. In the mythology of ancient ___, the Titans were a race of gods who ruled until they were overthrown by the Olympian gods.

Hieroglyphics (Hieroglyphs)

1. The ancient Egyptians wrote in ___.

2. A cartouche was an oval figure that surrounded a royal or divine name written in ancient Egyptian ___.

Homer

1. This Greek poet is believed to have lived in the eighth century bce.

2. The Greek epic poems the *Iliad* and the *Odyssey* are attributed to this author.

Inca

1. The ___ Empire was the largest empire in Pre-Columbian America. It was located in South America.

2. The ___ worshiped many gods. According to ___ mythology, Viracocha was the creator.

Maya

1. The ___ were the only Pre-Columbian Mesoamerican civilization with a fully developed written language.

2. Tikal in Guatemala and Chichén-Itzá in Mexico were two important centers of the ___.

Mesoamerican

1. This refers to the Pre-Columbian people living in the southern parts of North America, such as central Mexico, Guatemala, Nicaragua and Honduras.

2. ___ cultures included the Aztecs, the Maya and the Olmecs.

Mesopotamia

1. Bronze-Age ___ included the Sumer, Akkadian, Babylonian & Assyrian empires.

2. This region is often called "The Cradle of Civilization." The name means "The Land Between Two Rivers." The rivers are the Tigris and the Euphrates.

Mythology

1. It is a body of stories that tell about the world view of a culture.

2. It is a collection of stories that tell about the gods, goddesses, demigods and heroes of a culture.

Mummification

1. It was the ancient Egyptian method of preserving a body.

2. It involved embalming the body and wrapping it in linen.

Nile River

1. It was important to the ancient Egyptians because it created a fertile valley in the desert.

2. Most people of ancient Egypt settled near it because its flooding provided water for their crops.

Norse

1. Odin is the most important god in Scandinavian, or ___, mythology.

2. In ___ mythology the Aesir was the main race of gods; they lived in Asgard. They sometimes fought with the other race of gods known as the *vanir.*

Olympian Gods

1. These gods of ancient Greece ruled after the Titans were overthrown.

2. They include Zeus, Poseidon, Athena, Hera, Demeter, Ares, Apollo, Aphrodite, Hermes, Artemis, Hephaestus & Dionysus.

(NOTE: Not all sources include Hephaestus and Dionysus and some include Hestia and Hades.)

Olympic Games

1. Only free men who spoke Greek were allowed to compete in the ancient ones.

2. The ancient ones were held only in Olympia.

Osiris

1. After ___ was killed by his jealous brother Set, Isis resurrected him.

2. According to one version of the Egyptian legend, ___ became god of the underworld. He took over the job of judging the dead from Anubis.

Parthenon

1. It is located on the Acropolis in Athens.

2. It was built under the rule of the Greek statesman Pericles.

Persephone

1. In ancient Greek mythology, she was Demeter's daughter and wife of Hades.

2. According to the myth, she had to stay with Hades part of the year because she had eaten some pomegranate seeds while in the kingdom of Hades.

Pharaoh

1. The title given to rulers of ancient Egypt.

2. Ramesses II is thought by many to have been the most powerful ___ of ancient Egypt.

Philosopher(s)

1. The Greek ___ Socrates tried to get people to think by asking them questions calling for logical thinking.

2. Socrates, Plato and Aristotle are considered the most important ___ of ancient Greece.

Polytheistic

1. This refers to cultures that worship many gods. An antonym is *monotheistic.*

2. The ancient Egyptians, ancient Greeks and ancient Romans all had ___ belief systems. Judaism, Christianity and Islam are monotheistic.

Pompeii

1. This town near the Bay of Naples in Italy was destroyed by the eruption of Mt. Vesuvius.

2. This town was buried in mineral deposits when Mt. Vesuvius erupted in 79 CE.

Ancient Civilizations Bingo

Poseidon	**Pyramids**
1. In the mythology of the ancient Greeks, this Olympic god was god of the sea. 2. He was brother to Zeus and Hades. His Roman counterpart was Neptune.	1. These massive structures served as tombs for the pharaohs. 2. The Valley of the Kings contains many ___, including that of Tutankhamen.
Quetzalcoatl	**Ra**
1. It is the Aztec name for the feathered-serpent god of ancient Mesoamerica. 2. The name of this Mesoamerican god is a combination of the word for a brightly colored bird, and the word for serpent.	1. He was the sun god in the mythology of the ancient Egyptians. 2. According to the myth, this sun god was swallowed by Nut, the sky goddess, every evening and then reborn in the morning.
Roman Forum	**Song Dynasty**
1. It was the religious, political and economic center of ancient Rome. 2. Located near the Colosseum, it served as a public square where people could gather.	1. The Tang Dynasty, the ___ and the Ming Dynasty are together called the "Golden Age of China." 2. During the 1,000-year ___ gunpowder, the compass and printing were invented. Also, paper money came into use.
Terracotta Army	**Thor**
1. This refers to the 1000's of life-size soldiers and 100's of chariots and horses that were found buried near X'ian, China. 2. Construction of the ___ was ordered by Qin Shi Huang and buried with him upon his death.	1. He is the god of thunder in Norse mythology. 2. This Norse god had a hammer named Mjolnir.
Trojan War	**Zeus**
1. In Greek mythology this was caused by the abduction of Helen by Paris. 2. The *Iliad* was set on the ninth and final year of the ___. The ancient Greeks thought it was a historical event.	1. In ancient Greek mythology he is the supreme ruler of the Olympian gods. His Roman counterpart was Jupiter. 2. His wife was Hera. He was father to the Greek mythological heroes Perseus and Heracles.

Ancient Civilizations Bingo

Inca	Great Wall of China	Ra	Trojan War	Song Dynasty
Aztec	Aphrodite	Thor	Norse	Homer
Pompeii	Pharaoh		Mesoamerican	Olympic Games
Zeus	Acropolis	Forbidden City	Poseidon	Maya
Mesopotamia	City-state	Book of the Dead	Egypt	Gladiators

Ancient Civilizations Bingo

Zeus	Pyramids	Mummification	Osiris	Mesopotamia
Maya	Norse	Aqueducts	Acropolis	Polytheistic
Persephone	City-state		Chichén-Itzá	Forbidden City
Dynasties	Quetzalcoatl	Pharaoh	Mythology	Homer
Gladiators	Thor	Book of the Dead	Aztec	Egypt

Ancient Civilizations Bingo: Card No. 2

Ancient Civilizations Bingo

Zeus	Forbidden City	Norse	Poseidon	Pompeii
City-state	Aphrodite	Athens	Great Wall of China	Hieroglyphics (Hieroglyphs)
Acropolis	Thor		Polytheistic	Archeology
Pharaoh	Persephone	Mesopotamia	Dynasties	Mummification
Egypt	Aztec	Book of the Dead	Mythology	Ra

Ancient Civilizations Bingo

Pharaoh	Polytheistic	Mesopotamia	Aztec	Ra
Nile River	Aqueducts	Great Wall of China	Osiris	Pompeii
Mesoamerican	Dynasties		Song Dynasty	Trojan War
Forbidden City	Philosopher(s)	Thor	Book of the Dead	Athens
Greece	Gladiators	Olympian Gods	Egypt	Olympic Games

Ancient Civilizations Bingo

Gladiators	Song Dynasty	Acropolis	Aqueducts	Aztec
Nile River	Forbidden City	Athens	Chichén-Itzá	Aphrodite
Pyramids	Olympic Games		Circus	Colosseum
Homer	Polytheistic	Inca	Mythology	Greece
Norse	Book of the Dead	Philosopher(s)	Pharaoh	Mesoamerican

Ancient Civilizations Bingo: Card No. 5

Ancient Civilizations Bingo

Archeology	Polytheistic	Mummification	Pyramids	Olympic Games
Poseidon	Acropolis	Greece	Great Wall of China	Pompeii
Osiris	Athens		Aqueducts	Chichén-Itzá
Book of the Dead	Mesopotamia	Mythology	Olympian Gods	Mesoamerican
Maya	Forbidden City	Inca	Ra	Philosopher(s)

Ancient Civilizations Bingo: Card No. 6

Ancient Civilizations Bingo

Inca	Polytheistic	Colosseum	Circus	Norse
Maya	Ra	City-state	Aphrodite	Nile River
Mummification	Trojan War		Chichén-Itzá	Artifacts
Pharaoh	Dynasties	Pompeii	Zeus	Persephone
Book of the Dead	Aztec	Mythology	Olympian Gods	Archeology

Ancient Civilizations Bingo

Mesoamerican	Polytheistic	Augustus	Poseidon	Artifacts
Nile River	Pyramids	Osiris	Olympic Games	Aqueducts
Pompeii	Parthenon		Ra	Song Dynasty
Egypt	Pharaoh	Zeus	Greece	Dynasties
Thor	Book of the Dead	Olympian Gods	Acropolis	Maya

Ancient Civilizations Bingo

Chichén-Itzá	Norse	City-state	Pompeii	Olympic Games
Greece	Pyramids	Mesoamerican	Acropolis	Ra
Hieroglyphics (Hieroglyphs)	Inca		Aphrodite	Augustus
Artifacts	Gladiators	Mesopotamia	Circus	Colosseum
Dynasties	Mythology	Athens	Zeus	Song Dynasty

Ancient Civilizations Bingo

Zeus	Poseidon	Aqueducts	Osiris	Philosopher(s)
Olympic Games	Artifacts	Great Wall of China	Aphrodite	Ra
Parthenon	Polytheistic		Trojan War	Persephone
Mesopotamia	Homer	Greece	Mythology	Hieroglyphics (Hieroglyphs)
Athena	Maya	Mummification	Gladiators	Mesoamerican

Ancient Civilizations Bingo: Card No. 10

Ancient Civilizations Bingo

Archeology	Polytheistic	Acropolis	Greece	Maya
Augustus	Hieroglyphics (Hieroglyphs)	Circus	Chichén-Itzá	Great Wall of China
Nile River	Pyramids		Mummification	City-state
Athena	Pompeii	Mythology	Aztec	Zeus
Athens	Book of the Dead	Inca	Olympian Gods	Norse

Ancient Civilizations Bingo

Ancient Civilizations Bingo

Norse	Song Dynasty	Hieroglyphics (Hieroglyphs)	Poseidon	Chichén-Itzá
City-state	Thor	Pyramids	Olympian Gods	Aphrodite
Inca	Colosseum		Olympic Games	Osiris
Book of the Dead	Dynasties	Ra	Zeus	Nile River
Polytheistic	Augustus	Parthenon	Athens	Artifacts

Ancient Civilizations Bingo

Athena	Song Dynasty	Archeology	Hieroglyphics (Hieroglyphs)	Olympic Games
Pyramids	Augustus	Polytheistic	Chichén-Itzá	Persephone
Poseidon	Aqueducts		City-state	Colosseum
Mesoamerican	Mythology	Artifacts	Parthenon	Zeus
Book of the Dead	Homer	Olympian Gods	Inca	Circus

Ancient Civilizations Bingo

Aztec	Pyramids	Acropolis	Chichén-Itzá	Athena
Artifacts	Inca	Hieroglyphics (Hieroglyphs)	Aphrodite	Polytheistic
Greece	Trojan War		Mummification	Athens
Homer	Mythology	Parthenon	Aqueducts	Archeology
Book of the Dead	Osiris	Persephone	Maya	Mesoamerican

Ancient Civilizations Bingo: Card No. 14

Ancient Civilizations Bingo

Circus	Chichén-Itzá	Acropolis	Norse	Poseidon
Archeology	Mummification	Great Wall of China	Pyramids	Greece
Olympic Games	Inca		Pompeii	Ra
Book of the Dead	Hieroglyphics (Hieroglyphs)	Augustus	Mythology	Athena
Maya	Dynasties	Olympian Gods	Philosopher(s)	City-state

Ancient Civilizations Bingo: Card No. 15

© Barbara M. Peller

Ancient Civilizations Bingo

Aqueducts	Hieroglyphics (Hieroglyphs)	Augustus	Philosopher(s)	Quetzalcoatl
Osiris	Persephone	Colosseum	Nile River	Trojan War
Athena	Song Dynasty		Olympic Games	City-state
Pharaoh	Artifacts	Book of the Dead	Circus	Zeus
Greece	Terracotta Army	Olympian Gods	Dynasties	Polytheistic

Ancient Civilizations Bingo

Athena	Roman Forum	Confucius	Hieroglyphics (Hieroglyphs)	Aztec
Circus	Greece	Mythology	Trojan War	Colosseum
Chichén-Itzá	Zeus		Terracotta Army	Augustus
Gladiators	Maya	Mesoamerican	Acropolis	Persephone
Mesopotamia	Athens	Norse	Poseidon	Song Dynasty

Ancient Civilizations Bingo

Philosopher(s)	Parthenon	Artifacts	Greece	Osiris
Polytheistic	Athena	Mesopotamia	Olympic Games	Athens
Chichén-Itzá	Persephone		Confucius	Ra
Gladiators	Great Wall of China	Mythology	Zeus	Mummification
Terracotta Army	Hieroglyphics (Hieroglyphs)	Acropolis	Roman Forum	Archeology

Ancient Civilizations Bingo

c Games	Archeology	Hieroglyphics (Hieroglyphs)	Augustus	Parthenon
Circus	Poseidon	Ra	Norse	Trojan War
Roman Forum	Aztec		Aphrodite	Philosopher(s)
Mummification	Terracotta Army	Mesopotamia	Dynasties	Confucius
Pompeii	Quetzalcoatl	Maya	Mesoamerican	Olympian Gods

Ancient Civilizations Bingo

Parthenon	Roman Forum	Poseidon	Hieroglyphics (Hieroglyphs)	Aphrodite
Aqueducts	City-state	Nile River	Mesopotamia	Osiris
Song Dynasty	Colosseum		Pharaoh	Great Wall of China
Gladiators	Mesoamerican	Egypt	Dynasties	Terracotta Army
Forbidden City	Thor	Quetzalcoatl	Zeus	Confucius

Ancient Civilizations Bingo

Circus	Archeology	Nile River	Hieroglyphics (Hieroglyphs)	Homer
Song Dynasty	Confucius	Artifacts	Augustus	Inca
Persephone	Maya		Roman Forum	Acropolis
Mesopotamia	Norse	Terracotta Army	Gladiators	Mesoamerican
Pharaoh	Quetzalcoatl	Olympian Gods	Athena	Dynasties

Ancient
Civilizations
Bingo

Ancient Civilizations Bingo

Pompeii	Mummification	Confucius	Pyramids	Athena
Osiris	Poseidon	Philosopher(s)	Augustus	Aphrodite
Artifacts	Trojan War		Inca	Colosseum
Terracotta Army	Gladiators	Dynasties	Great Wall of China	Aztec
Quetzalcoatl	Athens	Roman Forum	Persephone	Nile River

Ancient Civilizations Bingo: Card No. 22

Ancient Civilizations Bingo

Aqueducts	Roman Forum	Norse	Pyramids	Olympian Gods
Archeology	Parthenon	Maya	Circus	Great Wall of China
Mummification	Athena		Egypt	Inca
Persephone	Quetzalcoatl	Terracotta Army	Athens	Dynasties
Homer	Mesoamerican	Thor	Mesopotamia	Confucius

Ancient Civilizations Bingo: Card No. 23

Ancient Civilizations Bingo

Aqueducts	Parthenon	Aztec	Roman Forum	Augustus
Olympic Games	Olympian Gods	Nile River	Osiris	Inca
Colosseum	Philosopher(s)		Athena	Persephone
Homer	Egypt	Terracotta Army	Athens	Song Dynasty
Forbidden City	Pharaoh	Quetzalcoatl	Poseidon	Thor

Ancient Civilizations Bingo

Pharaoh	Nile River	Roman Forum	Acropolis	Confucius
Great Wall of China	Homer	Circus	Aqueducts	Aphrodite
Song Dynasty	Augustus		Egypt	Terracotta Army
Philosopher(s)	Gladiators	Thor	Quetzalcoatl	Trojan War
Olympian Gods	Aztec	Artifacts	Greece	Forbidden City

Ancient Civilizations Bingo

Confucius	Roman Forum	Egypt	Osiris	Philosopher(s)
Mesopotamia	Poseidon	Augustus	Parthenon	Aqueducts
Homer	Mummification		Trojan War	Pharaoh
Athena	Pyramids	Gladiators	Quetzalcoatl	Terracotta Army
Colosseum	Greece	Acropolis	Thor	Forbidden City

Ancient Civilizations Bingo

Egypt	Artifacts	Roman Forum	Parthenon	City-state
Homer	Mummification	Circus	Terracotta Army	Aphrodite
Mythology	Thor		Quetzalcoatl	Pharaoh
Philosopher(s)	Archeology	Nile River	Forbidden City	Great Wall of China
Athena	Trojan War	Confucius	Pompeii	Colosseum

Ancient Civilizations Bingo

Olympic Games	Parthenon	Zeus	Roman Forum	Artifacts
City-state	Confucius	Egypt	Mesopotamia	Trojan War
Thor	Persephone		Philosopher(s)	Osiris
Colosseum	Pompeii	Maya	Quetzalcoatl	Terracotta Army
Pyramids	Chichén-Itzá	Athena	Forbidden City	Homer

Ancient Civilizations Bingo

Confucius	Parthenon	Philosopher(s)	Circus	Chichén-Itzá
Homer	Mesopotamia	Nile River	Colosseum	Pompeii
Song Dynasty	Egypt		Aphrodite	Roman Forum
City-state	Gladiators	Ra	Quetzalcoatl	Terracotta Army
Aqueducts	Augustus	Forbidden City	Archeology	Thor

Ancient Civilizations Bingo

Aztec	Roman Forum	Osiris	Chichén-Itzá	Terracotta Army
Great Wall of China	Ra	Mummification	Trojan War	Aphrodite
Forbidden City	Athens		Colosseum	Nile River
Homer	Archeology	Parthenon	Quetzalcoatl	Egypt
Gladiators	Norse	Thor	Confucius	Philosopher(s)